JAZZ PLAY ALONG

Book and CD for B♭, E♭ and C Instruments

Rodgers & Hart Classics

10 Rodgers & Hart Classics

Arranged and Produced
by Mark Taylor

T0058930

BOOK

CD

WILLIAMSON MUSIC is a registered trademark of the Family Trust u/w Richard Rodgers, the Family Trust u/w Dorothy F. Rodgers and the Estate of Oscar Hammerstein II

Performance Disclaimer:

ISBN 0-634-06141-0

WILLIAMSON MUSIC®
A RODGERS AND HAMMERSTEIN COMPANY
www.williamsonmusic.com

EXCLUSIVELY DISTRIBUTED BY

HAL•LEONARD®
CORPORATION
7777 W. BLUEMOUND RD. P.O. BOX 13819 MILWAUKEE, WI 53213

Visit Hal Leonard Online at
www.halleonard.com

Rodgers & Hart Classics

 JAZZ PLAY ALONG

Arranged and Produced by
Mark Taylor

Featured Players:

Graham Breedlove-Trumpet
John Desalme-Tenor Sax
Tony Nalker-Piano
Jim Roberts-Bass
Steve Fidyk-Drums

Recorded at Bias Studios, Springfield, Virginia
Bob Dawson, Engineer

HOW TO USE THE CD:

Each song has two tracks:

1) Split Track/Melody

Woodwind, Brass, Keyboard, and **Mallet Players** can use this track as a learning tool for melody, style and inflection.

Bass Players can learn and perform with this track – remove the recorded bass track by turning down the volume on the LEFT channel.

Keyboard and **Guitar Players** can learn and perform with this track – remove the recorded piano part by turning down the volume on the RIGHT channel.

2) Full Stereo Track

Soloists or **Groups** can learn and perform with this accompaniment track with the RHYTHM SECTION only.

MOUNTAIN GREENERY

FROM THE BROADWAY MUSICAL THE GARRICK GAIETIES

WORDS BY LORENZ HART
MUSIC BY RICHARD RODGERS

SOLOS (2 X'S)
2
C6/9 A+7 Dmi7 G7 C6/E Ami7 Dmi7 G7(b9)
1.
C6/9 Eb13(#11) Ami7/D D9 G9sus G+9
2.
F#mi7(b5) Fmi7 C6/E Eb9(#11) Dmi9 Db9(#11) C9 Gb9
F6 Gmi7 C9 F6 Bb9
Ami9 D9sus D7(b9) Dmi7 G9
C6/9 A+7 Dmi7 G7 C6/E Ami7 Dmi7 G7(b9)
D.S. AL CODA
LAST TIME
WITH REPEAT
C6/9 Eb13(#11) Dmi9 G+7(b9) C6/9 G+9
mf
CODA
Db9 C9(#11)

THIS CAN'T BE LOVE
FROM THE BOYS FROM SYRACUSE

WORDS BY LORENZ HART
MUSIC BY RICHARD RODGERS

CD
3 : SPLIT TRACK/MELODY
4 : FULL STEREO TRACK

C VERSION

SOLOS (2 X'S)

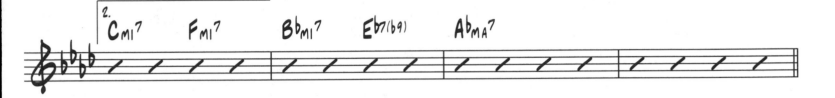

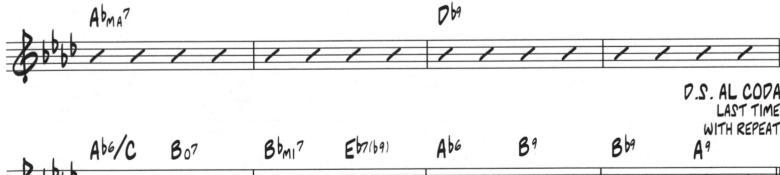

D.S. AL CODA
LAST TIME
WITH REPEAT

CODA

UNISON

CD
⑤ : SPLIT TRACK/MELODY
⑥ : FULL STEREO TRACK

C VERSION

FALLING IN LOVE WITH LOVE
FROM THE BOYS FROM SYRACUSE

WORDS BY LORENZ HART
MUSIC BY RICHARD RODGERS

SOLOS

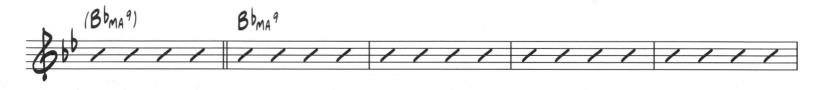

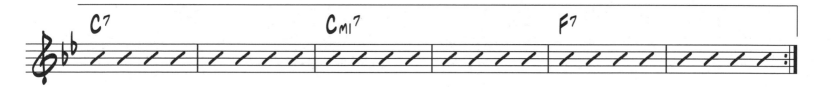

D.S. AL CODA
WITH REPEAT

MY FUNNY VALENTINE
FROM BABES IN ARMS

WORDS BY LORENZ HART
MUSIC BY RICHARD RODGERS

ISN'T IT ROMANTIC?

FROM THE PARAMOUNT PICTURE LOVE ME TONIGHT

WORDS BY LORENZ HART
MUSIC BY RICHARD RODGERS

CD
11 : SPLIT TRACK/MELODY
12 : FULL STEREO TRACK

C VERSION

THOU SWELL
FROM A CONNECTICUT YANKEE
FROM WORDS AND MUSIC

WORDS BY LORENZ HART
MUSIC BY RICHARD RODGERS

CD
13 : SPLIT TRACK/MELODY
14 : FULL STEREO TRACK

MANHATTAN
FROM THE BROADWAY MUSICAL THE GARRICK GAIETIES

WORDS BY LORENZ HART
MUSIC BY RICHARD RODGERS

C VERSION

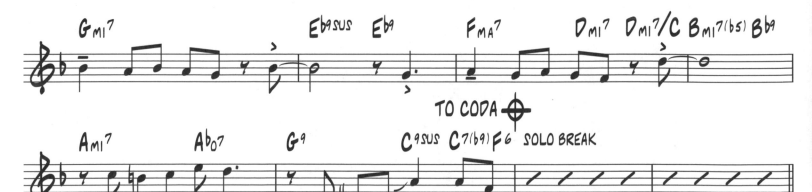

15

SOLOS

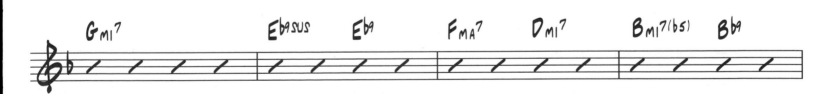

D.C. AL CODA

CD
15 : SPLIT TRACK/MELODY
16 : FULL STEREO TRACK

C VERSION

MY HEART STOOD STILL

FROM A CONNECTICUT YANKEE

WORDS BY LORENZ HART
MUSIC BY RICHARD RODGERS

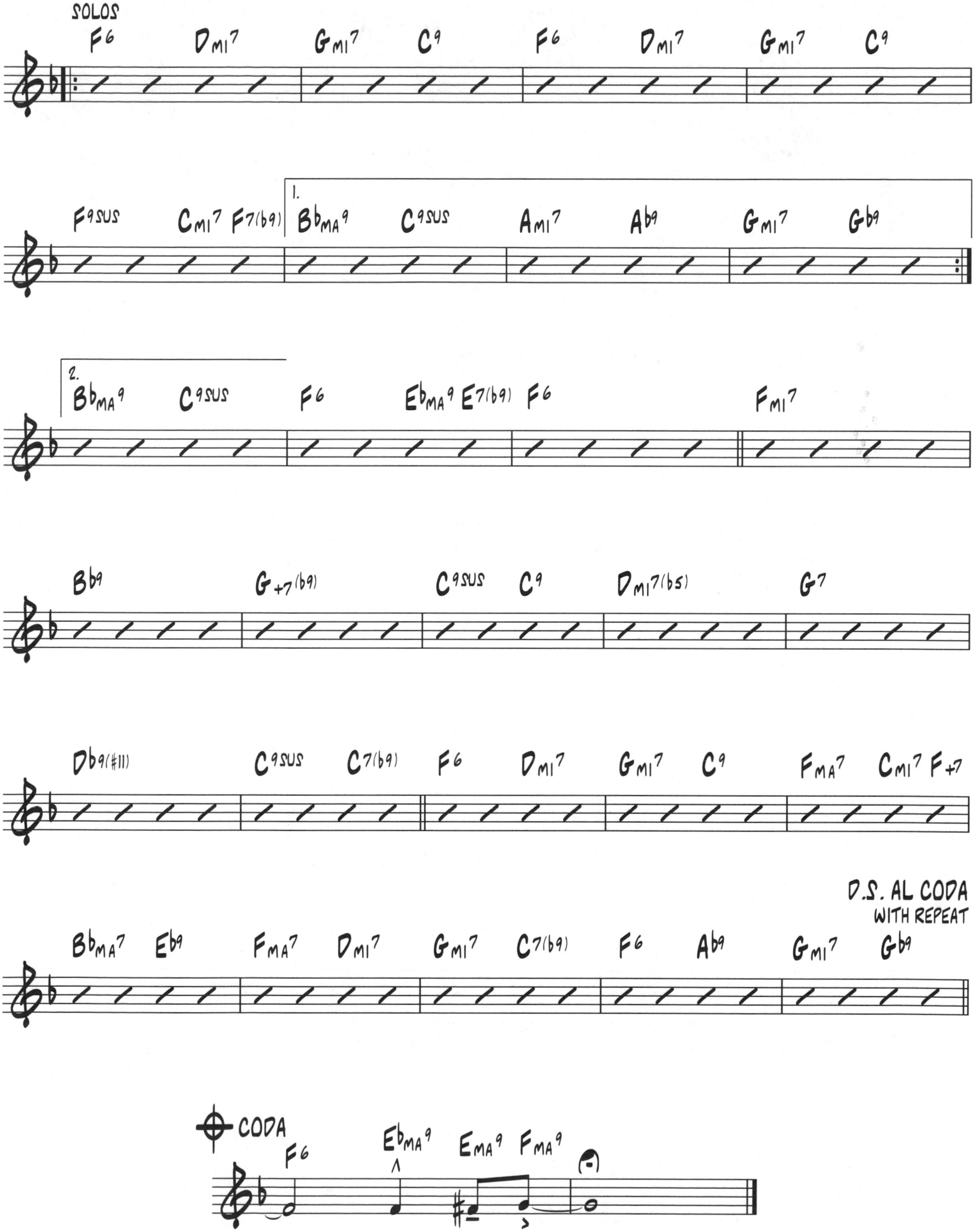
SOLOS
F6 DMI7 GMI7 C9 F6 DMI7 GMI7 C9
F9SUS CMI7 F7(b9)
1.
BbMA9 C9SUS AMI7 Ab9 GMI7 Gb9
2.
BbMA9 C9SUS F6 EbMA9 E7(b9) F6 FMI7
Bb9 G+7(b9) C9SUS C9 DMI7(b5) G7
Db9(#11) C9SUS C7(b9) F6 DMI7 GMI7 C9 FMA7 CMI7 F+7
D.S. AL CODA
WITH REPEAT
BbMA7 Eb9 FMA7 DMI7 GMI7 C7(b9) F6 Ab9 GMI7 Gb9
CODA
F6 EbMA9 EMA9 FMA9

WHERE OR WHEN
FROM BABES IN ARMS

WORDS BY LORENZ HART
MUSIC BY RICHARD RODGERS

CD
17: SPLIT TRACK/MELODY
18: FULL STEREO TRACK

C VERSION

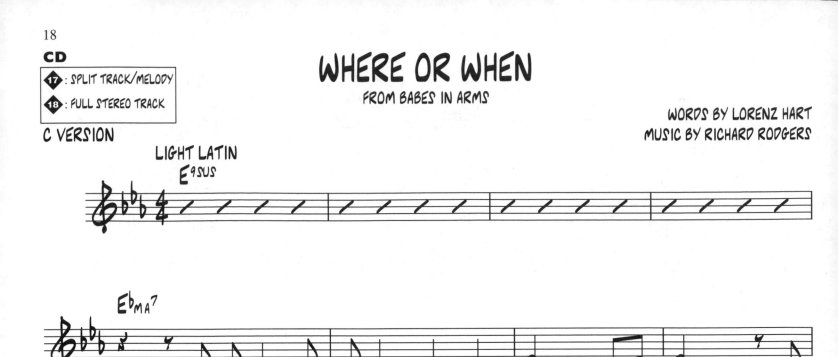

SOLOS

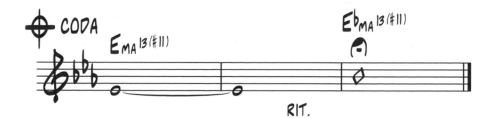

RIT.

YOU TOOK ADVANTAGE OF ME
FROM PRESENT ARMS

WORDS BY LORENZ HART
MUSIC BY RICHARD RODGERS

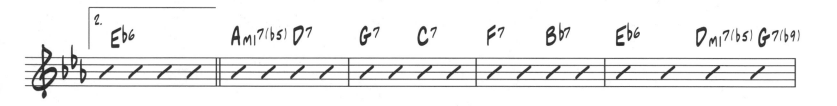

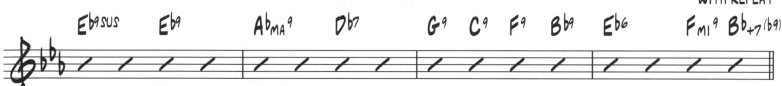

MOUNTAIN GREENERY
FROM THE BROADWAY MUSICAL THE GARRICK GAIETIES

WORDS BY LORENZ HART
MUSIC BY RICHARD RODGERS

Bb VERSION

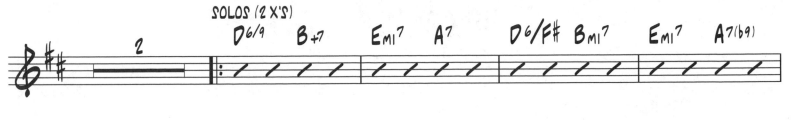

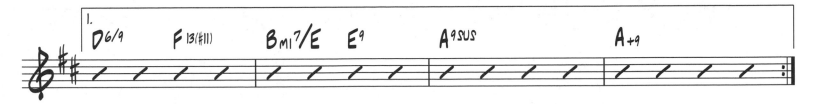

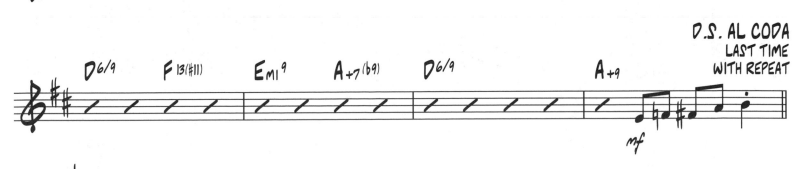

THIS CAN'T BE LOVE

FROM THE BOYS FROM SYRACUSE

CD
- 3 : SPLIT TRACK/MELODY
- 4 : FULL STEREO TRACK

Bb VERSION

WORDS BY LORENZ HART
MUSIC BY RICHARD RODGERS

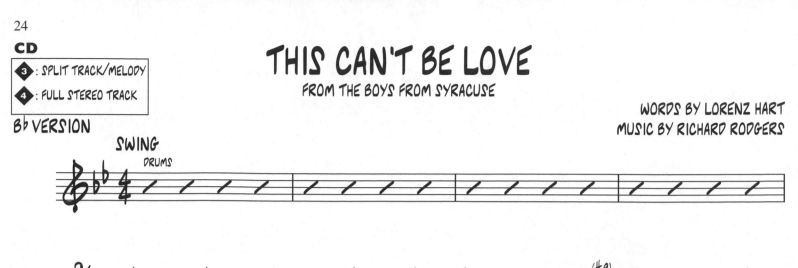

TO CODA ⊕

SOLOS (2 X'S)

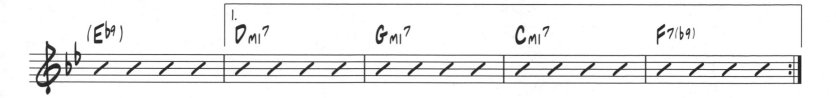

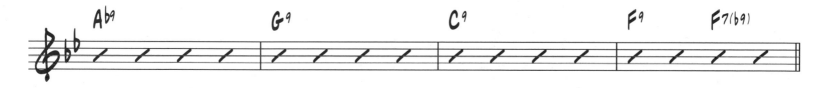

D.S. AL CODA
LAST TIME
WITH REPEAT

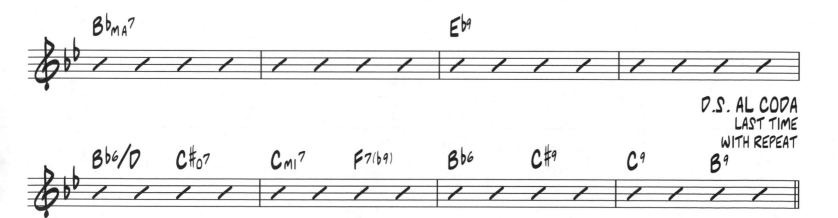

CODA

UNISON

FALLING IN LOVE WITH LOVE

FROM THE BOYS FROM SYRACUSE

WORDS BY LORENZ HART
MUSIC BY RICHARD RODGERS

Bb VERSION

MY FUNNY VALENTINE
FROM BABES IN ARMS

WORDS BY LORENZ HART
MUSIC BY RICHARD RODGERS

Bb VERSION

SOLOS   LATIN DBL X FEEL

Fma7/C   Emi7(b5) A7(b9)   Dmi   Dmi/C#   Dmi7/C   Dmi6/B

Bbma7   Gmi7   Emi7(b5)   A7(b9)   Dmi

Dmi/C#   Dmi7/C   Dmi6/B   Bbma7   Gmi7

Gmi7(b5)   C9sus   C13(b9)   Fma7/C   Gmi7/C   Fma7/C   Gmi7/C

Fma7/C Gmi7/C Fma7/C Gmi7/C Fma7   E+7(b9) A7(b9)   Dmi7   C#13 Cmi9 F7(b9)

Bbma7   Emi7(b5) A7(b9)   Dmi   Dmi(ma7)   Dmi7   Dmi6

                                                                    BALLAD
Bbma7   Emi7(b5) A7(b9)   Dmi7   G7(#9)(#5)   Cmi7   B13(#11) Bbma7   Ami7   Ab7(b9)
                                                                            mf

Gmi7   C7(b9)   Fma7/C   Gmi7/C   Fma7/C   Gmi7/C   Fma9(#11)
RIT.   A TEMPO

ISN'T IT ROMANTIC?

FROM THE PARAMOUNT PICTURE LOVE ME TONIGHT

WORDS BY LORENZ HART
MUSIC BY RICHARD RODGERS

THOU SWELL

FROM A CONNECTICUT YANKEE
FROM WORDS AND MUSIC

WORDS BY LORENZ HART
MUSIC BY RICHARD RODGERS

B♭ VERSION

MANHATTAN
FROM THE BROADWAY MUSICAL THE GARRICK GAIETIES

CD
13 : SPLIT TRACK/MELODY
14 : FULL STEREO TRACK

Bb VERSION

WORDS BY LORENZ HART
MUSIC BY RICHARD RODGERS

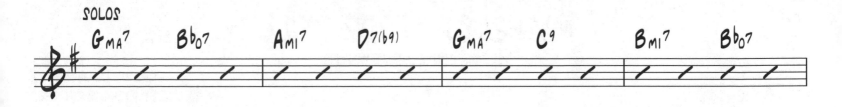

MY HEART STOOD STILL
FROM A CONNECTICUT YANKEE

WORDS BY LORENZ HART
MUSIC BY RICHARD RODGERS

CD
15: SPLIT TRACK/MELODY
16: FULL STEREO TRACK

B♭ VERSION

SOLOS

| G⁶ | Emi⁷ | Ami⁷ | D⁹ | G⁶ | Emi⁷ | Ami⁷ | D⁹ |

| G⁹sus | Dmi⁷ G⁷⁽ᵇ⁹⁾ | 1. Cma⁹ | D⁹sus | Bmi⁷ | Bᵇ⁹ | Ami⁷ | Aᵇ⁹ |

| 2. Cma⁹ | D⁹sus | G⁶ | Fma⁹ F#⁷⁽ᵇ⁹⁾ G⁶ | | | Gmi⁷ |

| C⁹ | A₊⁷⁽ᵇ⁹⁾ | D⁹sus D⁹ | Emi⁷⁽ᵇ⁵⁾ | A⁷ |

| Eᵇ⁹⁽#¹¹⁾ | D⁹sus D⁷⁽ᵇ⁹⁾ | G⁶ Emi⁷ | Ami⁷ D⁹ | Gma⁷ Dmi⁷ G₊⁷ |

D.S. AL CODA
WITH REPEAT

| Cma⁷ F⁹ | Gma⁷ Emi⁷ | Ami⁷ D⁷⁽ᵇ⁹⁾ | G⁶ Bᵇ⁹ | Ami⁷ Aᵇ⁹ |

⊕ CODA

G⁶   Fma⁹   F#ma⁹ Gma⁹

WHERE OR WHEN

FROM BABES IN ARMS

WORDS BY LORENZ HART
MUSIC BY RICHARD RODGERS

CD

17: SPLIT TRACK/MELODY
18: FULL STEREO TRACK

Bb VERSION

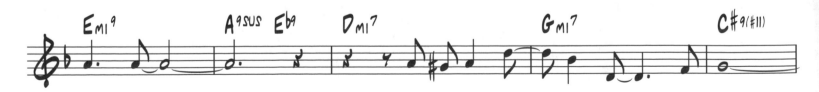

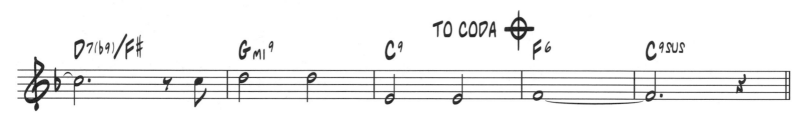

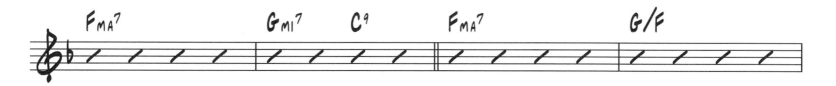

YOU TOOK ADVANTAGE OF ME
FROM PRESENT ARMS

CD
19 : SPLIT TRACK/MELODY
20 : FULL STEREO TRACK

Bb VERSION

WORDS BY LORENZ HART
MUSIC BY RICHARD RODGERS

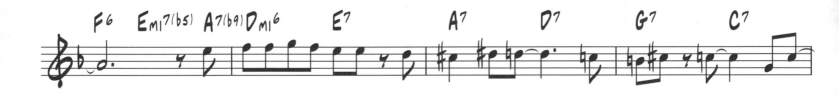

SOLOS

FMA7	F#o7	Gmi7	C7	Ami7	G#o7	Gmi7	C7

F9SUS	F9	BbMA9	Eb7	A9 D9 G9 C9	1. F6	C+7(b9)

2. | F6 | Bmi7(b5) E7 | A7 | D7 | G7 | C7 | F6 | Emi7(b5) A7(b9) |
| --- | --- | --- | --- | --- | --- | --- | --- |

Dmi6	E7	A7	D7	G7	C7	F6	Gmi9 C+7(b9)

FMA7	F#o7	Gmi7	C7	Ami7	G#o7	Gmi7	C7

D.S. AL CODA
WITH REPEAT

F9SUS	F9	BbMA9	Eb7	A9 D9 G9 C9	F6	Gmi9 C+7(b9)

MOUNTAIN GREENERY
FROM THE BROADWAY MUSICAL THE GARRICK GAIETIES

WORDS BY LORENZ HART
MUSIC BY RICHARD RODGERS

CD
1 : SPLIT TRACK/MELODY
2 : FULL STEREO TRACK

E♭ VERSION

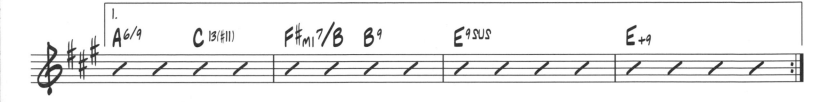

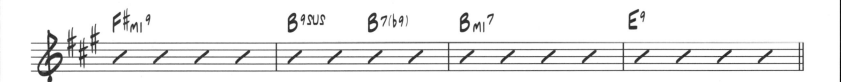

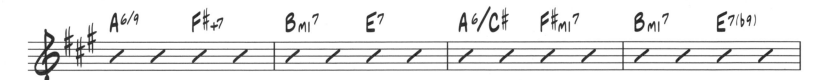

THIS CAN'T BE LOVE
FROM THE BOYS FROM SYRACUSE

WORDS BY LORENZ HART
MUSIC BY RICHARD RODGERS

CD
3: SPLIT TRACK/MELODY
4: FULL STEREO TRACK

Eb VERSION

SOLOS (2 X'S)

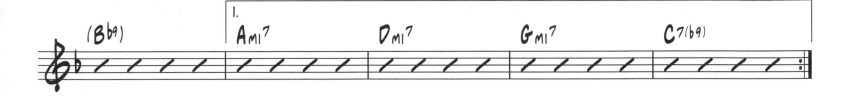

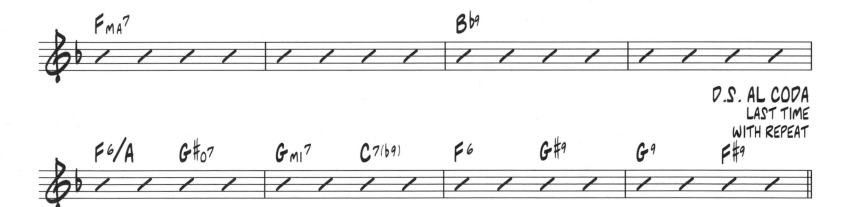

D.S. AL CODA
LAST TIME
WITH REPEAT

CODA
UNISON

CD
5 : SPLIT TRACK/MELODY
6 : FULL STEREO TRACK

FALLING IN LOVE WITH LOVE

FROM THE BOYS FROM SYRACUSE

WORDS BY LORENZ HART
MUSIC BY RICHARD RODGERS

Eb VERSION

SOLOS

G_{MA}9 | C_{MA}7 | B_{MI}7 | E7(b9) | A_{MI}7

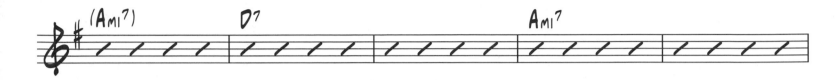

(A_{MI}7) | D7 | A_{MI}7

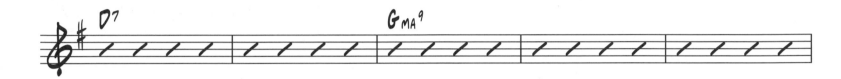

D7 | G_{MA}9

(G_{MA}9) | G_{MA}9

1.

F#_{MI}9 | B7 | E_{MI}7

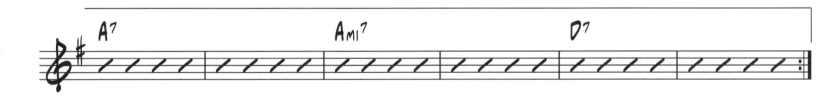

A7 | A_{MI}7 | D7

2.

F9 | B_{MI}9/E | E7(b9) | C_{MA}7 | B_{MI}7

D.S. AL CODA
WITH REPEAT

A_{MI}7 | D7 | G_{MA}9 | A_{MI}7 | D9

CODA
3 X'S

G_{MA}9 | A_{MI}9/G | G_{MA}9 | A_{MI}9/G | G#_{MA}9

MY FUNNY VALENTINE
FROM BABES IN ARMS

WORDS BY LORENZ HART
MUSIC BY RICHARD RODGERS

Eb VERSION

SOLOS   LATIN DBL X FEEL

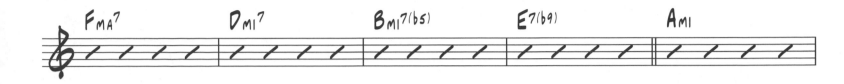

Line 1: Cᴍᴀ7/G | Bᴍɪ7(b5) E7(b9) | Aᴍɪ | Aᴍɪ/G# | Aᴍɪ7/G | Aᴍɪ6/F#

Line 2: Fᴍᴀ7 | Dᴍɪ7 | Bᴍɪ7(b5) | E7(b9) ‖ Aᴍɪ

Line 3: Aᴍɪ/G# | Aᴍɪ7/G | Aᴍɪ6/F# | Fᴍᴀ7 | Dᴍɪ7

Line 4: Dᴍɪ7(b5) | G9ꜱᴜꜱ G13(b9) | Cᴍᴀ7/G Dᴍɪ7/G | Cᴍᴀ7/G Dᴍɪ7/G

Line 5: Cᴍᴀ7/G Dᴍɪ7/G Cᴍᴀ7/G Dᴍɪ7/G | Cᴍᴀ7 B+7(b9) E7(b9) | Aᴍɪ7 G#13 Gᴍɪ9 C7(b9)

Line 6: Fᴍᴀ7 | Bᴍɪ7(b5) E7(b9) | Aᴍɪ | Aᴍɪ(ᴍᴀ7) | Aᴍɪ7 | Aᴍɪ6

BALLAD

Line 7: Fᴍᴀ7 | Bᴍɪ7(b5) E7(b9) | Aᴍɪ7 D7(#9)(#5) | Gᴍɪ7 F#13(#11) ‖ Fᴍᴀ7 | Eᴍɪ7 | Eb7(b9)

mf

Line 8: Dᴍɪ7 G7(b9) | Cᴍᴀ7/G Dᴍɪ7/G | Cᴍᴀ7/G Dᴍɪ7/G | Cᴍᴀ9(#11)

RIT.   A TEMPO

ISN'T IT ROMANTIC?
FROM THE PARAMOUNT PICTURE LOVE ME TONIGHT

WORDS BY LORENZ HART
MUSIC BY RICHARD RODGERS

THOU SWELL

FROM A CONNECTICUT YANKEE
FROM WORDS AND MUSIC

WORDS BY LORENZ HART
MUSIC BY RICHARD RODGERS

SOLOS

| Dma7 | Fo7 | Emi7 | A7(b9) | Dma7 | G9 | F#mi7 | Fo7 |

| Emi9 | | A9 | G9(#11) | F#mi7 | B7(b9) | Emi7 | A9 |

| Dma7 | Fo7 | Emi7 | A9 | A#o | Bmi9 | | G9 | F#9 | F9 |

| E9 | | | | Emi7 | A9 | Bb7(#9) | A9 |

| Dma7 | Fo7 | Emi7 | A7(b9) | Dma7 | G9 | F#mi7 | Fo7 |

| Emi9 | | A13 | G13(#11) | F#mi7 | C13(#11) | B9sus | B7(b9) |

| Emi7 | | C9sus | C9 | Dma7 | Bmi7 | G#mi7(b5) | G9 |

D.C. AL CODA

| F#mi7 | Fo7 | E9 | A7(b9) | D6 | B7(b9) | Emi7 | A7(b9) |

⊕ CODA

Eb9

D6/9

MY HEART STOOD STILL

FROM A CONNECTICUT YANKEE

WORDS BY LORENZ HART
MUSIC BY RICHARD RODGERS

SOLOS

| D⁶ | Bₘᵢ⁷ | Eₘᵢ⁷ | A⁹ | D⁶ | Bₘᵢ⁷ | Eₘᵢ⁷ | A⁹ |

| D⁹ˢᵘˢ | Aₘᵢ⁷ D⁷⁽ᵇ⁹⁾ | 1. Gₘₐ⁹ | A⁹ˢᵘˢ | F#ₘᵢ⁷ | F⁹ | Eₘᵢ⁷ | Eᵇ⁹ |

| 2. Gₘₐ⁹ | A⁹ˢᵘˢ | D⁶ | Cₘₐ⁹ C#⁷⁽ᵇ⁹⁾ D⁶ | Dₘᵢ⁷ |

| G⁹ | E₊₇⁽ᵇ⁹⁾ | A⁹ˢᵘˢ A⁹ | Bₘᵢ⁷⁽ᵇ⁵⁾ | E⁷ |

| Bᵇ⁹⁽#¹¹⁾ | A⁹ˢᵘˢ A⁷⁽ᵇ⁹⁾ | D⁶ Bₘᵢ⁷ | Eₘᵢ⁷ A⁹ | Dₘₐ⁷ Aₘᵢ⁷ D₊⁷ |

D.S. AL CODA
WITH REPEAT

| Gₘₐ⁷ C⁹ | Dₘₐ⁷ Bₘᵢ⁷ | Eₘᵢ⁷ A⁷⁽ᵇ⁹⁾ | D⁶ F⁹ | Eₘᵢ⁷ Eᵇ⁹ |

⊕ CODA

| D⁶ | Cₘₐ⁹ | C#ₘₐ⁹ Dₘₐ⁹ |

WHERE OR WHEN
FROM BABES IN ARMS

WORDS BY LORENZ HART
MUSIC BY RICHARD RODGERS

CD
17: SPLIT TRACK/MELODY
18: FULL STEREO TRACK

E♭ VERSION

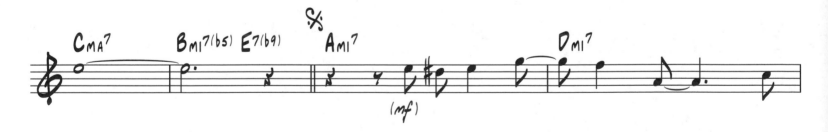

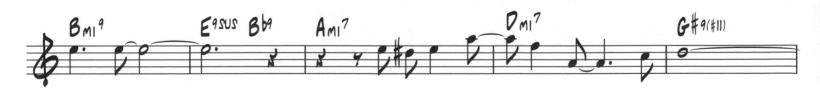

RIT.

You Took Advantage of Me
FROM PRESENT ARMS

WORDS BY LORENZ HART
MUSIC BY RICHARD RODGERS

Eb VERSION

MEDIUM SWING

SOLOS

| C$_{MA}$7 | C#$_{07}$ | D$_{MI}$7 | G7 | E$_{MI}$7 | D#$_{07}$ | D$_{MI}$7 | G7 |

| C9SUS | C9 | F$_{MA}$9 | B♭7 | E9 A9 D9 G9 | 1. C6 | G$_{+7}$(♭9) |

| 2. C6 | F#$_{MI}$7(♭5) B7 | E7 A7 | D7 G7 | C6 B$_{MI}$7(♭5) E7(♭9) |

| A$_{MI}$6 B7 | E7 A7 | D7 G7 | C6 D$_{MI}$9 G$_{+7}$(♭9) |

| C$_{MA}$7 C#$_{07}$ | D$_{MI}$7 G7 | E$_{MI}$7 D#$_{07}$ | D$_{MI}$7 G7 |

D.S. AL CODA
WITH REPEAT

| C9SUS C9 | F$_{MA}$9 B♭7 | E9 A9 D9 G9 | C6 D$_{MI}$9 G$_{+7}$(♭9) |

CODA

E9 A9 D9 G7 C6 F9 E9 A9 D9 G7 C6 A$_{+7}$(#9)

D9 G9 DRUMS C7(#9) C7(#9)

MOUNTAIN GREENERY
FROM THE BROADWAY MUSICAL THE GARRICK GAIETIES

WORDS BY LORENZ HART
MUSIC BY RICHARD RODGERS

THIS CAN'T BE LOVE
FROM THE BOYS FROM SYRACUSE

WORDS BY LORENZ HART
MUSIC BY RICHARD RODGERS

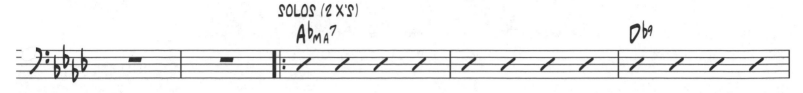

SOLOS (2 X'S)

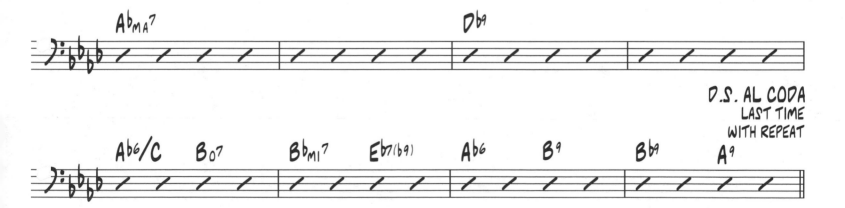

D.S. AL CODA
LAST TIME
WITH REPEAT

SOLOS

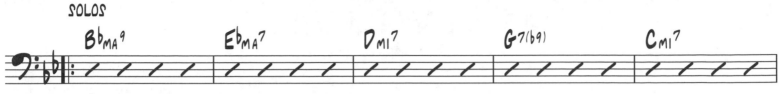

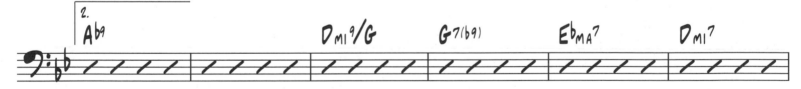

D.S. AL CODA
WITH REPEAT

MY FUNNY VALENTINE
FROM BABES IN ARMS

WORDS BY LORENZ HART
MUSIC BY RICHARD RODGERS

ISN'T IT ROMANTIC?
FROM THE PARAMOUNT PICTURE LOVE ME TONIGHT

WORDS BY LORENZ HART
MUSIC BY RICHARD RODGERS

THOU SWELL

FROM A CONNECTICUT YANKEE
FROM WORDS AND MUSIC

WORDS BY LORENZ HART
MUSIC BY RICHARD RODGERS

MANHATTAN
FROM THE BROADWAY MUSICAL THE GARRICK GAIETIES

WORDS BY LORENZ HART
MUSIC BY RICHARD RODGERS

SOLOS

D.C. AL CODA

MY HEART STOOD STILL

FROM A CONNECTICUT YANKEE

WORDS BY LORENZ HART
MUSIC BY RICHARD RODGERS

SOLOS

F6   Dmi7   Gmi7   C9   F6   Dmi7   Gmi7   C9

F9sus   Cmi7 F7(b9)   1. Bbma9   C9sus   Ami7   Ab9   Gmi7   Gb9

2. Bbma9   C9sus   F6   Ebma9 E7(b9) F6   Fmi7

Bb9   G+7(b9)   C9sus   C9   Dmi7(b5)   G7

Db9(#11)   C9sus   C7(b9)   F6   Dmi7   Gmi7   C9   Fma7   Cmi7 F+7

D.S. AL CODA
WITH REPEAT

Bbma7   Eb9   Fma7   Dmi7   Gmi7   C7(b9)   F6   Ab9   Gmi7   Gb9

CODA   F6   Ebma9   Ema9   Fma9

WHERE OR WHEN
FROM BABES IN ARMS

WORDS BY LORENZ HART
MUSIC BY RICHARD RODGERS

RIT.

You Took Advantage Of Me
FROM PRESENT ARMS

WORDS BY LORENZ HART
MUSIC BY RICHARD RODGERS

CD
19 : SPLIT TRACK/MELODY
20 : FULL STEREO TRACK

C VERSION

MEDIUM SWING

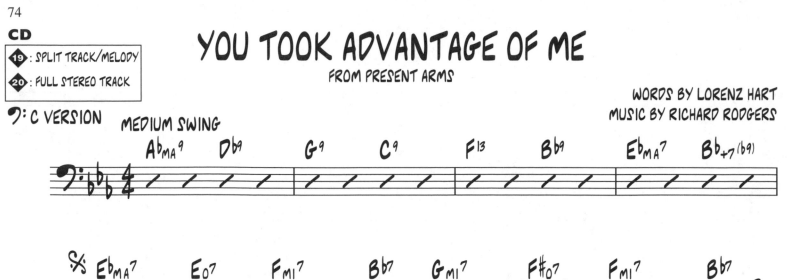

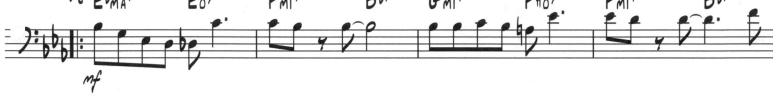

TO CODA

SOLOS

| Eb MA7 | E O7 | F MI7 | Bb7 | G MI7 | F# O7 | F MI7 | Bb7 |

| Eb9 SUS | Eb9 | Ab MA9 | Db7 | G9 C9 F9 Bb9 | 1. Eb6 | Bb+7(b9) |

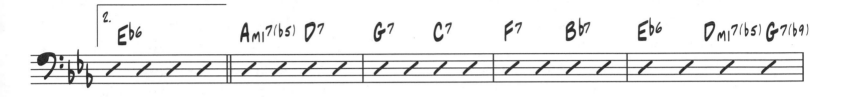

| 2. Eb6 | A MI7(b5) D7 | G7 C7 | F7 Bb7 | Eb6 D MI7(b5) G7(b9) |

| C MI6 D7 | G7 C7 | F7 Bb7 | Eb6 F MI9 Bb+7(b9) |

| Eb MA7 E O7 | F MI7 Bb7 | G MI7 F# O7 | F MI7 Bb7 |

D.S. AL CODA
WITH REPEAT

| Eb9 SUS Eb9 | Ab MA9 Db7 | G9 C9 F9 Bb9 | Eb6 F MI9 Bb+7(b9) |

CODA G9 C9 F9 Bb7 Eb6 Ab9 G9 C9 F9 Bb7 Eb6 C+7(#9)

F9 Bb9 DRUMS Eb7(#9) Eb7(#9)

Lyrics

FALLING IN LOVE WITH LOVE

I weave with brightly colored strings
To keep my mind off other things;
So, ladies, let your fingers dance,
And keep your hands out of romance.
Lovely witches,
Let the stitches
Keep your fingers under control.
Cut the thread, but leave
The whole heart whole.
Merry maids can sew and sleep;
Wives can only sew and weep!
refrain:
Falling in love with love
Is falling for make-believe.
Falling in love with love
Is playing the fool.
Caring too much is such
A juvenile fancy.
Learning to trust is just
For children in school.
I fell in love with love
One night when the moon was full.
I was unwise, with eyes
Unable to see.
I fell in love with love,
With love everlasting,
But love fell out with me.

MY FUNNY VALENTINE

Behold the way our fine-feathered friend
His virtue doth parade.
Though knowest not, my dim-witted friend,
The picture thou hast made.
Thy vacant brow and thy tousled hair
Conceal thy good intent.
Thou noble, upright, truthful, sincere,
And slightly dopey gent, you're
My funny Valentine,
Sweet comic Valentine,
You make me smile with my heart.
Your looks are laughable,
Unphotographable,
Yet you're my favorite work of art.
Is your figure less than Greek?
Is your mouth a little weak?
When you open it to speak
Are you smart?
But don't change a hair for me,
Not if you care for me,
Stay, little Valentine, stay!
Each day is Valentine's Day.

WHERE OR WHEN

When you're awake, the things you think
Come from the dreams you dream.
Thought has wings, and lots of things
Are seldom what they seem.
Sometimes you think you've lived before
All that you live today.
Things you do come back to you,
As though they knew the way.
Oh, the tricks the mind can play!
It seems we stood and talked like this before,
We looked at each other
In the same way then,
But I can't remember where or when.
The clothes you're wearing
Are the clothes you wore,
The smile you are smiling
You were smiling then.
But I can't remember where or when.
Some things that happen, for the first time
Seem to be happening again.
And so it seems that we have met before,
And laughed before, and loved before.
But who knows where or when!

ISN'T IT ROMANTIC?

verse:
I've never met you,
Yet never doubt, dear,
I can't forget you
I've thought you out, dear.
I know your profile
And I know the way you kiss:
Just the thing I miss
On a night like this.
If dreams are made of
Imagination,
I'm not afraid of
My own creation.
With all my heart,
My heart is here for you to take.
Why should I quake?
I'm not awake.

refrain:
Isn't it romantic?
Music in the night
A dream that can be heard.
Isn't it romantic?
Moving shadows write
The oldest magic word.
I hear the breezes playing
In the trees above,
While all the world is saying,
"You were meant for love."
Isn't it romantic?
Merely to be young
On such a night as this.
Isn't it romantic.
Every note that's sung
Is like a lover's kiss.
Sweet symbols in the moonlight,
Do you mean that I will fall
In love, perchance?
Isn't it romance?

*verse 2 (from the film):**
My face is glowing,
I'm energetic,
The art of sewing,
I found poetic.
My needle punctuates the rhythm of
romance!
I don't give a stitch
If I don't get rich.
A custom tailor
Who has no custom,
Is like a sailor,
No one will trust 'em.
But there is magic
In the music of my shears;
I shed no tears.
Lend me your ears!

refrain 2 (from the film):
Isn't it romantic?
Soon I will have found
Some girl that I adore.
Isn't it romantic?
While I sit around,
My love can scrub the floor.
She'll kiss me every hour,
Or she'll get the sack.
And when I take a shower
She can scrub my back.
Isn't it romantic?
On a moon-lit night
She'll cook me onion soup.
Kiddies are romantic
And if we don't fight,
We soon will have a troupe!
We'll help the population,
It's a duty that we owe
To dear old France.
Isn't it romance?

*In the film, the song is passed from character to character.

MANHATTAN

verse:
Summer journeys to Niagara
And to other places Aggra-
Vate all our cares.
We'll save our fares!
I've a cozy little flat in
What is known as Manhattan,
We'll settle down
Right here in town!
refrain:
We'll have Manhattan
The Bronx and Staten Island too.
It's lovely going through the zoo.
It's very fancy
On old Delancey Street, you know.
The subway charms us so
When balmy breezes blow
To and fro.
And tell me what street
Compares with Mott Street in July?
Sweet pushcarts gently gliding by.
The great big city's a wondrous toy
Just made for a girl and boy.
We'll turn Manhattan
Into an isle of joy.
We'll go to Greenwich,
Where modern men itch to be free;
And Bowling Green you'll see with me.
We'll bathe at Brighton;
The fish you'll frighten when you're in,
Your bathing suit so thin
Will make the shellfish grin
Fin to fin.
I'd like to take a
Sail on Jamaica Bay with you.
And fair Canarsie's Lake we'll view.
The city's bustle cannot destroy
The dreams of a girl and boy.
We'll turn Manhattan
Into an isle of joy.
We'll go to Yonkers
Where true love conquers in the wilds.

And starve together, dear, in Childs.
We'll go to Coney
And eat baloney on a roll.
In Central Park we'll stroll
Where our first kiss we stole,
Soul to soul.
Our future babies
We'll take to Abie's Irish Rose.
I hope they'll live to see it close.
The city's clamor can never spoil
The dreams of a boy and goil.
We'll turn Manhattan
Into an isle of joy.
We'll have Manhattan,
The Bronx and Staten Island too.
We'll try to cross Fifth Avenue.
As black as onyx
We'll find the Bronnix Park Express.
Our Flatbush flat, I guess,
Will be a great success,
More or less.
A short vacation
On Inspiration Point we'll spend,
And in the station house we'll end.
But Civic Virtue cannot destroy
The dreams of a girl and boy.
We'll turn Manhattan
Into an isle of joy.

MOUNTAIN GREENERY

He:
On the first of May
It is moving day;
Spring is here, so blow your job,
Throw your job away;
Now's the time to trust
To your wanderlust.
In the city's dust you wait,
Must you wait?
Just you wait:
In a mountain greenery,
Where God paints the scenery,
Just two crazy people together;
While you love your lover,
Let blue skies be your coverlet,
When it rains we'll laugh at the weather.
And if you're good
I'll search for wood,
So you can cook
While I stand looking.
Beans could get no keener reception
In a beanery,
Bless our mountain greenery home!

She:
Simple cooking means
More than French cuisines.
I've a banquet planned
Which is sandwiches and beans,
Coffee's just as grand
With a little sand.
Eat and you'll grow fatter, boy,
S'matter, boy?
'Atta boy!
In a mountain greenery,
Where God paints the scenery,
Just two crazy people together;
How we love sequestering
Where no pests are pestering,
No dear mama holds us in tether!

Mosquitoes here
Won't bite you, dear;
I'll let them sting
Me on the finger.
We could find no cleaner retreat
From life's machinery
Than our mountain greenery home!

He:
When the world was young,
Old Father Adam with sin would grapple,
So we're entitled to just one apple,
I mean to make applesauce.

She:
Underneath the bough,
We'll learn a lesson from Mister Omar;
Beneath the eyes of no Pa and no Ma,
Old Lady Nature is boss.

He:
Washing dishes,
Catching fishes
In the running stream,
We'll curse the smell o'
Citronella,
Even when we dream.

She:
Head upon the ground,
Your downy pillow is just a boulder.

He:
I'll have new dimples before I'm older;
But life is peaches and cream.
And if you're good,
I'll search for wood,
So you can cook.
While I stand looking.

Both:
Beans could get no keener reception
In a beanery.
Bless our mountain greenery home.

MY HEART STOOD STILL

Note: These are the original show lyrics.

Martin:
I laughed at sweethearts
I met at schools;
All indiscreet hearts
Seemed romantic fools.
A house in Iceland
Was my heart's domain.
I saw your eyes;
Now castles rise in Spain!
refrain:
I took one look at you,
That's all I meant to do,
And then my heart stood still!
My feet could step and walk,
My lips could move and talk,
And yet my heart stood still!
Though not a single word was spoken,
I could tell you knew,
That unfelt clasp of hands
Told me so well you knew.
I never lived at all
Until the thrill
Of that moment when
My heart stood still.
Sandy:
Through all my schooldays
I hated boys;
Those April Fool days
Brought me love-less joys.
I read my Plato,
Love I thought a sin;
But since your kiss,
I'm reading Missus Glynn!
refrain

THIS CAN'T BE LOVE

In Verona, my late cousin Romeo
Was three times as stupid as my Dromio.
For he fell in love
And then he died of it.
Poor half-wit!
refrain:
This can't be love
Because I feel so well;
No sobs, no sorrows, no sighs.
This can't be love,
I get no dizzy spell,
My head is not in the skies.
My heart does not stand still;
Just hear it beat!
This is too sweet
To be love.
This can't be love
Because I feel so well,
But still I love to look in your eyes.
Though your cousin
Loved my cousin Juliet,
Loved her with a passion
Much more truly yet,
Some poor playwright
Wrote their drama just for fun.
It won't run!
refrain

THOU SWELL

Babe, we are well met, as in a spell met;
I lift my helmet,
Sandy, you're just dandy.
For just this here lad.
You're such a fistful,
My eyes are mistful;
Are you too wistful to care?
Do say you care
To say, "Come near lad."
You are so graceful;
Have you wings?
You have a face full of nice things;
You have no speaking voice, dear,
With every word it sings.
refrain:
Thou swell! Thou witty!
Thou sweet! Thou grand!
Wouldst kiss me pretty?
Wouldst hold my hand?
Both thine eyes are cute too;
What they do to me.
Hear me holler
I choose a sweet lollapalooza in thee.
I'd feel so rich in a hut for two
Two rooms and kitchen
I'm sure would do;
Give me just a plot of,
Not a lot of land and,
Thou swell! Thou witty! Thou grand!
Thy words are queer, Sir,
Unto mine ear, Sir,
Yet thou'rt a dear, Sir, to me.
Thou could'st woo me.
Now could'st thou try, knight.
I'd murmur "Swell" too,
And like it well too.
More thou wilt tell to Sandy.
Thou art dandy;
Now art thou my knight.
Thine arms are martial, thou hast grace.
My cheek is partial to they face.
And if thy lips grow weary,
Mine are their resting place.
refrain

YOU TOOK ADVANTAGE OF ME

He:
In the spring
When the feeling was chronic,
And my caution was leaving you flat,
I should have made use of the tonic,
Before you gave me "that!"
A mental deficient you'll grade me,
I've given you plenty of data.
You came, you saw and you slayed me,
And that-a is that-a!
refrain:
I'm a sentimental sap, that's all.
What's the use of trying not to fall?
I have no will,
You've made your kill,
'Cause you took advantage of me!
I'm just like an apple on a bough,
And you're gonna shake me down
Somehow,
So what's the use,
You've cooked my goose,
'Cause you took advantage of me!
I'm so hot and bothered that I don't know
My elbow from my ear;
I suffer something awful each time you go,
And much worse when you're near.
Here am I with all my bridges burned,
Just a babe in arms
Where you're concerned,
So lock the doors and call me your's
'Cause you took advantage of me!
She:
When a girl has the heart of a mother
It must go to someone of course;
It can't be a sister or brother
And so I loved my horse.
But horses are frequently silly,
Mine ran from the beach of Kaluta,
And left me alone for a filly,
So I-a picked you-a.
refrain